On
Cosmopolitanism and Forgiveness

Praise for the series

'. . . allows a space for distinguished thinkers to write about their passions.'

The Philosophers' Magazine

'. . . deserve high praise.'

Boyd Tonkin, The Independent (UK)

'This is clearly an important series. I look forward to reading future volumes.'

Frank Kermode, author of Shakespeare's Language

'. . . both rigorous and accessible.'

Humanist News

'. . . the series looks superb.'

Quentin Skinner

'. . . an excellent and beautiful series.'

Ben Rogers, author of A.J. Ayer: A Life

'Routledge's *Thinking in Action* series is the theory junkie's answer to the eminently pocketable Penguin 60s series.'

Mute Magazine (UK)

'Routledge's new series, *Thinking in Action*, brings philosophers to our aid . . .'

The Evening Standard (UK)

'. . . a welcome new series by Routledge.'

Bulletin of Science, Technology and Society (Can)

JACQUES DERRIDA

Translated by Mark Dooley and
Michael Hughes

With a preface by Simon Critchley and
Richard Kearney

On
Cosmopolitanism and
Forgiveness

Routledge
Taylor & Francis Group

LONDON AND NEW YORK

'On Cosmopolitanism' first published 1997 in French as 'Cosmopolites de tous
les pays, encore un effort!'
by Editions Galilée, 9 rue Linée, 75006 Paris, France

English translation as 'On Cosmopolitanism' first published 2001
by Routledge
2 Park Square, Milton Park, Abingdon, Oxon, OX14 4RN

Simultaneously published in the USA and Canada
by Routledge
270 Madison Ave, New York, NY 10016

Reprinted 2001, 2003 (twice), 2004, 2005, 2006 (twice), 2007 (three times),
2008, 2009 and 2010

Routledge is an imprint of the Taylor & Francis Group, an informa business

Typeset in Joanna by RefineCatch Limited, Bungay, Suffolk
Printed and bound in Great Britain by TJ International Ltd, Padstow, Cornwall

British Library Cataloguing in Publication Data
A catalogue record for this book is available from the British Library

Library of Congress Cataloging in Publication Data
Derrida, Jacques.
    [Cosmopolites de tous les pays, encore un effort. English]
    On cosmopolitanism and forgiveness / Jacques Derrida.
      p. cm. – (Thinking in action)
    1. Refugees. 2. Asylum, Right of. 3. Internationalism. 4. Forgiveness. I. Title.
    II. Series.
JV6346 .D47 2001
320.01'1–dc21

2001016110

ISBN10: 0-415-22711-9 (hbk)
ISBN10: 0-415-22712-7 (pbk)
ISBN13: 978-0-415-22711-7 (hbk)
ISBN13: 978-0-415-22712-4 (pbk)

Preface

The two essays in this volume are telling examples of Jacques Derrida's recent work on ethical and political issues. Both deal with pressing contemporary problems. First, Derrida discusses the dilemmas of reconciliation and amnesty in situations where the bloody traumas of history demand forms of forgiveness, such as Apartheid in South Africa, the Vichy Regime in France, or the current situation in Algeria. Second, Derrida addresses the dilemma of refugee and asylum rights, which is a theme also addressed, in a different mode, by Sir Michael Dummett in another volume in this series.

Both essays comprise a response by Derrida to a specific solicitation or set of questions. In the case of 'On Forgiveness', this takes the form of a considered address to a number of queries put to Derrida by a leading French intellectual journal, Le Monde des débats (December 1999). Derrida argues that true forgiveness consists in forgiving the unforgivable: a contradiction all the more acute in this century of war crimes (from the Holocaust, to Algeria, to Kosovo) and reconciliation tribunals, such as the Truth and Reconciliation Commission in South Africa. If forgiveness forgave only the forgivable, then, Derrida claims, the very idea of forgiveness would disappear. It has to consist in the attempt to forgive the unforgivable: whether the murderousness of Apartheid or the Shoah. Derrida's response, originally entitled 'Le Siècle et le pardon', is translated here by Michael Collins Hughes, in an edited version of the exchange, which retains, we hope, its original tone of vibrant immediacy.

The second essay, 'On Cosmopolitanism', is also a response to a particular request: in this instance, an invitation to address the International Parliament of Writers in Strasbourg in 1996, on the subject of cosmopolitan rights for asylum-seekers, refugees, and immigrants. Here Derrida revisits the perennial question of 'open cities' (ville franches) or 'refuge cities' (villes refuges) where migrants may seek sanctuary from the pressures of persecution, intimidation, and exile. The speech, entitled 'Cosmopolites de tous les pays, encore un effort!' when it was first published in French by Editions Galilée in 1997, is translated for this volume by Mark Dooley. Like 'On Forgiveness', this address bears the marks of its occasional origin and once more testifies to Derrida's characteristic readiness – in spite of persistently and perplexingly misguided charges of apathy and indifference – to tackle topics of major moral consequence for our times. 'On Forgiveness' and 'On Cosmopolitanism' are proof, if proof were needed, that deconstruction is not some obscure textual operation intimated in a mandarin prose style, but is a concrete intervention in contexts that is governed by an undeconstructable concern for justice.

The two texts are linked together by a common logic. What Derrida is seeking to do in much of his recent work might be described as the historical analysis of concepts, a form of conceptual genealogy. He selects a concept from what he always describes as 'the heritage' – let's call it the dominant Western tradition – and then proceeds, via an analysis that is at once historical, contextual, and thematic, to bring out the logic of that concept. If one looks back at Derrida's work over the past 15 years, one finds a whole bundle of such analyses, where he works on a range of key concepts: friendship, law, justice, testimony, the gift, hospitality, cosmopolitanism, forgiveness, and, most recently, the death penalty. The logic that Derrida identifies usually takes the form of a contradiction or a double imperative. In 'On Forgiveness', he asks characteristically, 'What does it mean when the heritage includes an injunction at once double and contradictory?'

Let's examine this procedure in relation to the text on cosmopolitanism. First, Derrida's text is an address to the International Parliament of Writers in 1996. This was a particularly dark year for France's reputation as a place of hospitality and refuge from oppression, with the clumsy and violent imposition of the Debret laws on immigrants and those without rights of residence, the so-called 'sans papiers', which provoked mass demonstrations of protest in Paris. In this highly charged political context, the demand of the International Parliament of Writers was for places or cities of refuge for immigrants. In order to address this emotive and contested issue, Derrida picks out the concept of cosmopolitanism, a concept that a country like France has been keen to adopt in fashioning its self-image of tolerance, openness, and hospitality. As ever, we see Derrida identifying a concept from the Western heritage in order to address critically a specific and concrete context. Then, with the help of a number of thinkers, notably Hannah Arendt and Kant, Derrida proceeds to dig out the logical structure behind the image of cosmopolitanism and question it. He locates a double or contradictory imperative within the concept of cosmopolitanism: on the one hand, there is an unconditional hospitality which should offer the right of refuge to all immigrants and newcomers. But on the other hand, hospitality has to be conditional: there has to be some limitation on rights of residence. All the *political* difficulty of immigration consists in negotiating between these two imperatives. Derrida's identification of a contradictory logic at the heart of the concept of cosmopolitanism is not staged in order to paralyse political action, but, on the contrary, in order to enable it.

We find the same logic at work in 'On Forgiveness'. First, Derrida identifies a certain globalisation of the concept of forgiveness in contexts that call for forms of 'national reconciliation', as when the Japanese Prime Minister asked forgiveness of the Koreans for past violence, or when, in South Africa, white oppressors asked forgiveness of their black victims. What is interesting here is the way in which the Abrahamic moral tradition, in which forgiveness is a central concept and which is at the basis of the three great monotheisms, has globalised itself in a more or less secular form. Increasingly, we live in a world where forgiveness is demanded, granted, or withheld.

Derrida then proceeds to pick out the logical structure of the concept of forgiveness, which has a characteristically double structure and which testifies to an equivocation in the Western heritage. He writes,

> It is important to analyse at its base the tension at the heart of a heritage between, *on the one side*, the idea which is also a demand for the *unconditioned*, gracious, infinite, aneconomic forgiveness granted *to the guilty as guilty*, without counterpart, even to those who do not repent or ask forgiveness, and *on the other side*, as a great number of texts testify through many semantic refinements and difficulties, a conditional forgiveness proportionate to the recognition of the fault, to repentance, to the transformation of the sinner who then explicitly asks for forgiveness.

So, as we saw above in the text on cosmopolitanism, it is a question of the negotiation between the unconditional and the conditional, between the absolute and the relative, between the universal and the particular. The logic of the concept of forgiveness is divided, then, between two poles. On the one hand, there is what Derrida calls an 'unconditional purity', which could be described as ethical in the Kantian sense of the Moral Law or the Levinasian sense of infinite responsibility. On the other hand, there is the order of pragmatic conditions, at once historical, legal, political, and quotidian, which demand that the unforgivable be forgiven, that the irreconcilable be reconciled.

It is important to point out that, for Derrida, these two orders of the unconditional and the conditional are also in a relation of contradiction, where they remain both irreducible to one another and indissociable. Derrida's closing thesis in 'On Forgiveness', which reverberates with increasing power across his work of the past 15 years, is that responsible political action and decision making consists in the negotiation between these two irreconcilable yet indissociable demands. On the one hand, pragmatic political or legal action has to be related to a moment of unconditionality or infinite responsibility if it is not going to be reduced to the prudential demands of the moment. Political action has to be based on a moment of universality that exceeds the pragmatic demands of the specific context. But, on the other hand, such unconditionality cannot, must not, Derrida insists, be permitted to programme political action, where decisions would be algorithmically deduced from incontestable ethical precepts. Just political action requires active respect for both poles of this tension. Derrida writes, 'I must then, and only then, respond to this transaction between two contradictory and equally justified imperatives.' We have to learn to forgive whilst knowing that true forgiveness only forgives the unforgivable. Justice must be restlessly negotiated in the conflict between these two imperatives. A justice that is always to be done.

Simon Critchley and
Richard Kearney

Part One
On Cosmopolitanism

Cosmopolitanism[1]

Where have we received the image of cosmopolitanism from? *And what is happening* to it? As for this citizen of the world, we do not know what the future holds in store for it. One must ask today whether we can still make a legitimate distinction between the two forms of the metropolis – the City and the State. Moreover, one is seeking to inquire if an International Parliament of Writers can still, as its name seems to suggest, find inspiration in what has been called, for more than twenty centuries now, cosmopolitanism. For is it not the case that cosmopolitanism has something to do either with all the cities or with all the states of the world? At a time when the 'end of the city' resonates as though it were a verdict, at a time when this diagnosis or prognosis is held by many, how can we still dream of a novel status for the city, and thus for the 'cities of refuge', through a *renewal* of international law? Let us not anticipate a simple response to such a question. It will be necessary therefore to proceed otherwise, particularly if one is tempted to think, as I do, that 'The Charter for the Cities of Refuge' and 'The International Agency for Cities of Refuge'

'On Cosmopolitanism', translated by Mark Dooley

which appear on our programme must open themselves up to something more and other than merely banal articles in the literature on international law. They must, if they are to succeed in so doing, make an audacious call for a genuine innovation in the history of the right to asylum or the duty to hospitality.

The name 'cities of refuge' appears to be inscribed in gold letters at the very heart of the constitution of the International Parliament of Writers. Ever since our first meeting, we have been calling for the opening of such refuge cities across the world. That, in effect, very much resembles a new cosmo-*politics*. We have undertaken to bring about the proclamation and institution of numerous and, above all, autonomous 'cities of refuge', each as independent from the other and from the state as possible, but, nevertheless, allied to each other according to forms of solidarity yet to be invented. This invention is our task; the theoretical or critical reflection it involves is indissociable from the practical initiatives we have already, out of a sense of urgency, initiated and implemented. Whether it be the foreigner in general, the immigrant, the exiled, the deported, the stateless or the displaced person (the task being as much to distinguish prudently between these categories as is possible), we would ask these new cities of refuge to reorient the politics of the state. We would ask them to transform and reform the modalities of membership by which the city (*cité*) belongs to the state, as in a developing Europe or in international juridical structures still dominated by the inviolable rule of state sovereignty – an intangible rule, or one at least supposed such, which is becoming increasingly precarious and problematic nonetheless. This should no longer be the ultimate horizon for cities of refuge. Is this possible?

In committing ourselves thus, in asking that metropolises and modest cities commit themselves in this way, in choosing for them the name of 'cities of refuge', we have doubtless meant more than one thing, as was the case for the name 'parliament'. In reviving the traditional meaning of an expression and in restoring a memorable heritage to its former dignity, we have been eager to propose simultaneously, beyond the old word, an original concept of hospitality, of the duty (*devoir*) of hospitality, and of the right (*droit*) to hospitality. What then would such a concept be? How might it be adapted to the pressing urgencies which summon and overwhelm us? How might it respond to unprecedented tragedies and injunctions which serve to constrain and hinder it?

I regret not having been present at the inauguration of this solemn meeting, but permit me, by way of saluting those here present, to evoke at least a vague outline of this new charter of hospitality and to sketch, albeit in an overly schematic way, its principal features. What in effect is the context in which we have proposed this new ethic or this new *cosmopolitics* of the cities of refuge? Is it necessary to call to mind the violence which rages on a worldwide scale? Is it still necessary to highlight the fact that such crimes sometimes bear the signature of state organisations or of non-state organisations? Is it possible to enumerate the multiplicity of menaces, of acts of censorship (*censure*) or of terrorism, of persecutions and of enslavements in all their forms? The victims of these are innumerable and nearly always anonymous, but increasingly they are what one refers to as intellectuals, scholars, journalists, and writers – men and women capable of speaking out (*porter une parole*) – in a public domain that the new powers of telecommunication render increasingly formidable – to the police forces of all countries, to the religious, political, economic, and social forces of censorship and repression, whether they be state-sponsored or not. Let us not proffer an example, for there are too many; and to cite the best known would risk sending the anonymous others back into the darkness (*mal*) from which they find it hard to escape, a darkness which is truly the worst and the condition of all others. If we look to the city, rather than to the state, it is because we have given up hope that the state might create a new image for the city. This should be elaborated and inscribed in our Statutes one day. Whenever the State is neither the foremost author of, nor the foremost guarantor against the violence which forces refugees or exiles to flee, it is often powerless to ensure the protection and the liberty of its own citizens before a terrorist menace, whether or not it has a religious or nationalist alibi. This is a phenomenon with a long historical sequence, one which Hannah Arendt has called, in a text which we should closely scrutinise, 'The Decline of the Nation-State and the End of the Rights of Man'.[2] Arendt proposes here, in particular, an analysis of the modern history of minorities, of those 'without a State', the *Heimatlosen*, of the stateless and homeless, and of deported and 'displaced persons'. She identifies *two great upheavals*, most notably between the two wars:

1 First, the progressive abolition, upon the arrival of hundreds of thousands of stateless people (*l'apatrides*), of a right to asylum which was 'the only right that had ever

figured as a symbol of Human Rights in the domain of international relations'. Arendt recalls that this right has a 'sacred history', and that it remains 'the only modern vestige of the medieval principle of *quid est in territorio est de territorio*' (p. 280). 'But', continues Arendt, 'although the right to asylum had continued to exist in a world organised into nation states, and though it had even, in some individual cases, survived two world wars, it is still felt to be an anachronism and a principle incompatible with the international laws of the State.' At the time when Arendt was writing this, *circa* 1950, she identified the absence in international charters of the right to asylum (for example in the Charter of the League of Nations). Things have doubtless evolved a little since then, as we shall see in a moment, but further transformations are still necessary.

2 The second upheaval (*choc*) in Europe was to follow a massive influx (*arrivée*) of refugees, which necessitated abandoning the classic recourse to repatriation or naturalisation. Indeed, we have still to create a satisfactory substitute for it. In describing at length the effects of these traumas, Arendt has perhaps identified one of our tasks and, at the very least, the background to our Charter and of our Statutes (*Statuts*). She does not speak of the city, but in the shadow of the two upheavals (*l'onde du double choc*) she describes and which she situates between the two wars, we must today pose new questions concerning the destiny of cities and the role which they might play in these unprecedented circumstances. How can the right to asylum be redefined and developed without repatriation and without naturalisation? Could the City, equipped with new rights and greater sovereignty, open

up new horizons of possibility previously undreamt of by international state law? For let us not hesitate to declare our ultimate ambition, what gives meaning to our project: our plea is for what we have decided to call the 'city of refuge'. This is not to suggest that we ought to restore an essentially classical concept of the city by giving it new attributes and powers; neither would it be simply a matter of endowing the old subject we call 'the city' with new predicates. No, we are dreaming of another concept, of another set of rights for the city, of another politics of the city. I am aware that this might appear utopian for a thousand reasons, but at the same time, as modest as it is, what we have already begun to do proves that something of this sort can, from now on, function – and this disjointed process cannot be dissociated from the turbulence which affects, over the lengthy duration of a process, the axioms of international law.

Is there thus any hope for cities exercising hospitality if we recognise with Arendt, as I feel we must, that nowadays international law is limited by treaties between sovereign states, and that not even a 'government of the world' would be capable of sorting things out? Arendt was writing of something the veracity of which still holds today:

> contrary to the best-intentioned humanitarian attempts to obtain new declarations of human rights from international organisations, it should be understood that this idea transcends the *present sphere of international law which still operates in terms of reciprocal agreements and treaties between sovereign states*; and, for the time being, a sphere that is above the nations does not exist. Furthermore, this

It would be necessary to expand upon and refine what she says of groups and individuals who, between the two wars, lost *all status* – not only their citizenship but even the title of 'stateless people'. We would also have to re-evaluate, in this regard, in Europe and elsewhere, the respective roles of States, Unions, Federations or State Confederations on the one hand, and of cities on the other. If the name and the identity of something like the city still has a meaning, could it, when dealing with the related questions of hospitality and refuge, elevate itself above nation-states or at least free itself from them (*s'affranchir*), in order to become, to coin a phrase in a new and novel way, a *free city* (*une ville franche*)? Under the exemption itself (*en général*), the statutes of immunity or exemption occasionally had attached to them, as in the case of the right to asylum, certain places (diplomatic or religious) to which one could retreat in order to escape from the threat of injustice.

Such might be the magnitude of our task, a theoretical task indissociable from its political implementation (*mise en œuvre*) – a task which is all the more imperative given that the situation is becoming ever more bleak with each passing day. As the figures show, the right to political asylum is less and less respected both in France and in Europe. Lately, there has been talk of a 'dark year for asylum seekers in France'.[4] Because of such understandable despondency, the number of applications for political asylum has been regularly diminishing. In fact, OFPRA (The French Office for the Protection of

Refugees and the Stateless) toughened its criteria and spectacularly reduced the number of refugees afforded asylum
status. The number of those whose application for asylum
has, I might add, continued to rise throughout the 1980s and
since the beginning of the 1990s.

Since the Revolution, France has had a certain tendency to
portray itself as being more open to political refugees in contra-
distinction to other European countries, but the motives
behind such a policy of opening up to the foreigner have,
however, never been 'ethical' *stricto sensu* – in the sense of the
moral law or the law of the land (*séjour*) – (*ethos*), or, indeed,
the law of hospitality. The comparative drop in the birth
rate in France since the middle of the eighteenth century
has generally permitted her to be more liberal in matters
of immigration for obvious economic reasons: when the
economy is doing well, and workers are needed, one tends
not to be overly particular when trying to sort out political
and economic motivations. This was especially true in the
1960s, when an economic boom resulted in a greater need
for immigrant workers. It is also worth noting that the right
to asylum has only recently become a specifically juridical
concept (*définitionelle*) and a positive juridical concept,
despite the fact that its spirit was already present in the French
Constitution. The Constitution of 1946 granted the right to
asylum only to those characterised as persons persecuted
because of their 'action in the name of liberty'. Even though it
subscribed to the Geneva Convention in 1951, it is only in
1954 that France was forced to broaden its definition of a
political refugee to encompass all persons forced into exile
because 'their lives or their liberties are found to be under

threat by reason of their race, religion, or political opinions'. Considerably broadened, it is true, but very recent nevertheless. Even the Geneva Convention was itself very limited in the manner in which it could be applied, and even at that we are still a long way from the idea of cosmopolitanism as defined in Kant's famous text on the right to (*droit de*) universal hospitality, the limits and restrictions of which I shall recall in just a moment. The Geneva Convention of 1951, which obliged France to improve its asylum laws, could only direct itself to 'events in Europe prior to 1951'. Much later, at the end of the 1960s, precisely at the time when there were signs of the beginning of a process which has dramatically deteriorated today, the area, place, and dates specified by the Geneva Convention (that is, the events in Europe prior to 1951) were enhanced by a particular protocol added to this convention in New York in 1967, and eventually extended to cover events occurring beyond Europe after 1951. (These are the developments which Hannah Arendt could neither have known about nor evoked when she was writing her text sometime around 1950.)

There is still a considerable gap separating the great and generous principles of the right to asylum inherited from the Enlightenment thinkers and from the French Revolution and, on the other hand, the historical reality or the effective implementation (*mise en œuvre*) of these principles. It is controlled, curbed, and monitored by implacable juridical restrictions; it is overseen by what the preface of a book on *The Crisis of the Right to Asylum in France* refers to as a 'mean-minded' juridical tradition.[5] In truth, if the juridical tradition remains 'mean-minded' and restrictive, it is because it is under the control of the demographico-economic interest – that is, the interest of the nation-state that regulates asylum. Refugee status ought not to be conflated with the status of an immigrant, not even of a political immigrant. It has happened that a recognition of refugee status, be it political or economic, has only come into effect long after entry into France. We shall have to maintain a close eye on these sometimes subtle distinctions between types of status, especially since the difference between the economic and the political now appears more problematic than ever.

Both to the right and to the left, French politicians speak of 'the control of immigration'. This forms part of the compulsory rhetoric of electoral programmes. Now, as Luc Legoux notes, the expression 'immigration control' means that asylum will be granted only to those who cannot expect the slightest economic benefit upon immigration. The absurdity of this condition is manifestly apparent: how can a purely political refugee claim to have been truly welcomed into a new settlement without that entailing some form of economic gain? He will of course have to work, for each individual seeking refuge cannot simply be placed in the care of the host country. This gives rise to an important consideration which our conventions will have to address: how can the hosts (*hôtes*) and guests of cities of refuge be helped to recreate, through work and creative activity, a living and durable network in new places and occasionally in a new language? This distinction between the economic and the political is not, therefore, merely abstract or gratuitous: it is truly hypocritical and perverse; it makes it virtually impossible ever to grant political asylum and even, in a sense, to apply the law, for in its implementation it would depend entirely on opportunistic considerations, occasionally electoral and political, which, in the last analysis, become a matter for the police, of real or imaginary security issues, of demography, and of the market. The discourse on the refugee, asylum or hospitality, thus risks becoming nothing but pure rhetorical alibis. As Legoux notes, 'what tends to render the asylum laws in France ineffectual for the people of poor countries is the result of a particular conception of asylum, one with a long and complex history, and one which is becoming ever more stringent'.[6]

This tendency to obstruct is extremely common, not to Europe in general (supposing that one had ever been able to speak of 'Europe' in general), but to the countries of the European Union; it is a price that is oftentimes paid as a consequence of the Schengen Agreement – the accords of which, Jacques Chirac declared, have not been, up to now at least, implemented in full by France. At a time when we claim to be lifting internal borders, we proceed to bolt the external borders of the European Union tightly. Asylum-seekers knock successively on each of the doors of the European Union states and end up being repelled at each one of them. Under the pretext of combating economic immigrants purporting to be exiles from political persecution, the states reject applications for the right to asylum more often than ever. Even when they do not do so in the form of an explicit and reasoned (motivée) juridical response, they often leave it to their police to enforce the law; one could cite the case of a Kurd to whom a French tribunal had officially granted the right to asylum, but who was nevertheless deported to Turkey by the police without a single protest. As in the case of many other examples, notably those to do with 'violations of hospitality', whereby those who had allegedly harboured political suspects were increasingly charged or indicted, one has to be mindful of the profound problem of the role and status of the police, of, in the first instance, border police, but also of a police without borders, without determinable limit, who from then on become all-pervasive and elusive, as Benjamin noted in *Critique of Violence* just after the First World War.

The police become omnipresent and spectral in the so-called civilised states once they undertake to *make the law*, instead of simply contenting themselves with applying it and seeing that it is observed. This fact becomes clearer than ever in an age of new teletechnologies. As Benjamin has already reminded us, in such an age police violence is both 'faceless' and 'formless', and is thus beyond all accountability. Nowhere is this violence, as such, to be found; in the civilised states, the spectre of its ghostly apparition extends itself limitlessly. It must be understood, of course, that we are concerned here with developing neither an unjust nor a utopian discourse of suspicion of the function of the police, especially in their fight against those crimes which do fall within their jurisdiction (such as terrorism, drug-trafficking, and the activities of mafias of all kinds). We are simply questioning the limits of police jurisdiction and the conditions in which it operates, particularly as far as foreigners are concerned.

With respect to new police powers (national or international), one is touching here on one of the most serious questions of law that a future elaboration of our charter for the cities of refuge would have to develop and inscribe throughout the course of an interminable struggle: it will be necessary to restrict the legal powers and scope of the police by giving them a purely administrative role under the strict control and regulation of certain political authorities, who will see to it that human rights and a more broadly defined right to asylum are respected.

Hannah Arendt, in the spirit of Benjamin, had already highlighted the new and increased powers afforded to the modern police to handle refugees. She did so after making a remark about anonymity and fame which we should, particularly in an International Parliament of Writers, take seriously:

> Only fame will eventually answer the repeated complaint of refugees of all social strata that 'nobody here knows who I am'; and it is true that the chances of the famous refugee are improved just as a dog with a name has a better chance to survive than a stray dog who is just a dog in general.
>
> The nation-state, incapable of providing a law for those who had lost the protection of a national government, transferred the whole matter to the police. This was the first time the police in Western Europe had received authority to act on its own, to rule directly over people; in one sphere of public life it was no longer an instrument to carry out and enforce the law, but had become a ruling authority independent of government and ministries.
>
> (p. 287)

We know only too well that today this problem is more serious than ever, and we could provide much evidence to this effect. A movement protesting against the charge of what has been called for some time now 'violations of hospitality' has been growing in France; certain organisations have taken control of it, and, more widely, the press has become its mouthpiece. A proposal of 'Toubon-law', in the spirit and beyond of the laws known as 'Pasqua', has now come on to the agenda. Under examination in the parliamentary assemblies, in the National Assembly and in the Senate, is a proposal to treat as acts of terrorism, or as 'participation in a criminal conspiracy', all hospitality accorded to 'foreigners' whose 'papers are not in order', or those simply 'without papers'. This project, in effect, makes even more draconian article 21 of the famous edict of 2 November 1945, which had already cited as a 'criminal act' all help given to foreigners whose papers were not in order. Hence, what was a criminal act is now in danger of becoming an 'act of terrorism'. Moreover, it appears that this plan is in direct contravention of the Schengen accords (ratified by France) – which permit a conviction of someone for giving help to a foreigner 'without papers' only if it can be proved that this person derived financial profit from such assistance.

We have doubtless chosen the term 'city of refuge' because, for quite specific historical reasons, it commands our respect, and also out of respect for those who cultivate an 'ethic of hospitality'. 'To cultivate an ethic of hospitality' – is such an expression not tautologous? Despite all the tensions or contradictions which distinguish it, and despite all the perversions that can befall it, one cannot speak of cultivating an ethic of hospitality. Hospitality is culture itself and not simply one ethic amongst others. Insofar as it has to do with the *ethos*, that is, the residence, one's home, the familiar place of dwelling, inasmuch as it is a manner of being there, the manner in which we relate to ourselves and to others, to others as our own or as foreigners, *ethics is hospitality*; ethics is so thoroughly coextensive with the experience of hospitality. But for this very reason, and because being at home with oneself (*l'être-soi chez soi* – *l'ipséité même* – the other within oneself) supposes a reception or inclusion of the other which one seeks to appropriate, control, and master according to different modalities of violence, there is a history of hospitality, an always possible perversion of the law of hospitality (which can appear unconditional), and of the laws which come to limit and condition it in its inscription as a law. It is from within this history that I would like to select, in a very tentative and preliminary way, some reference points which are of great significance to us here.

First, what we have been calling the city of refuge, it seems to me, bridges several traditions or several moments in Western, European, or para-European traditions. We shall recognise in the Hebraic tradition, on the one hand, those cities which would welcome and protect those innocents who sought refuge from what the texts of that time call 'bloody vengeance'. This urban right to immunity and to hospitality was rigorously and juridically developed and the text in which it first emerged was, without doubt, the Book of Numbers:[7] God ordered Moses to institute cities which would be, according to the very letter of the Bible itself, 'cities of refuge' or 'asylum', and to begin with there would be 'six cities of refuge', in particular for the 'resident alien, or temporary settler'. Two beautiful texts in French have been devoted to this Hebraic tradition of the city of refuge, and I would like to recall here that, from one generation to the other, both authors of these essays are philosophers associated with Strasbourg, with this generous border city, this eminently European city, the capital city of Europe, and the first of our refuge cities. I am speaking here of the meditations by Emmanuel Levinas in 'The Cities of Refuge' ['Les Villes-refuges', in *L'Au-delà du verset* (Minuit, 1982), p. 51], and by Daniel Payot in *Refuge Cities* [*Des villes-refuges, Témoignage et espacement* (Ed. de l'Aube, 1992), especially pp. 65ff.].

In the medieval tradition, on the other hand, one can identify a certain sovereignty of the city: the city itself could determine the laws of hospitality, the articles of predetermined law, both plural and restrictive, with which they meant to condition the Great Law of Hospitality – an unconditional Law, both singular and universal, which ordered that the borders be open to each and every one, to every other, to all who might come, without question or without their even having to identify who they are or whence they came. (It would be necessary to study what was called *sanctuary*, which was provided by the churches so as to secure immunity or survival for refugees, and by virtue of which they risked becoming enclaves; and also *auctoritas*, which allowed kings or lords to shield their guests (*hôtes*) from all those in pursuit; or, what occurred between the warring Italian cities when one became a place of refuge for the exiled, the refugee, and those banished from another city; and we who are reminded of writers in this context can call to mind a certain story about Dante, banished from Florence and then welcomed, it would seem, at Ravenna.)

Finally, at this juncture, we could identify the cosmopolitan (*cosmopolitique*) tradition common to a certain Greek stoicism and a Pauline Christianity, of which the inheritors were the figures of the Enlightenment, and to which Kant will doubtlessly have given the most rigorous philosophical formulation in his famous *Definitive Article in View of Perpetual Peace*: 'The law of cosmopolitanism must be restricted to the conditions of universal hospitality.' This is not the place to analyse this remarkable *Article*, or its immense historical context, which has been excised from this text without trace. It was Cicero who was to bequeath a certain Stoic cosmopolitanism. Pauline Christianity revived, radicalised and literally 'politicised' the primary injunctions of all the Abrahamic religions, since, for example, the 'Opening of the Gates of Israel' – which had, however, specified the restrictive conditions of hospitality so as to ensure the 'safety' or 'security' of the 'strong city' (26, 2). Saint Paul gives to these appeals or to these dictats their modern names. These are also theologico-political names, since they explicitly designate citizenship or world co-citizenship: 'no longer foreigners nor metic in a foreign land, but fellow-citizens with God's people, members of God's household' (Ephesians II. 19–20). In this sentence, 'foreigners' (*xenoi*) is also translated by guests (*hospites*); and 'metic' – but see also 'immigrants', for '*paroikoi*' – designates as much the neighbour, from a point of view which is important to us here, as the foreigner without political rights in another city or country. I am modifying and mixing several translations, including that of Chouraqui, but it will be necessary to analyse closely the political stakes and the theological implications of these questions of semantics; Grosjean-Leturmy's translation, in the Pléiade Library, for example, could literally announce the space of what we are interpreting as the 'city of refuge'. But that is precisely what I would like to begin putting into question here – i.e., the secularised version of such Pauline cosmopolitanism: 'And so therefore, you are no longer foreigners abroad (*xenoi, hospites*), you are fellow-citizens of the Saints, you belong to the House of God' (*sympolitai tōn hagiōn kai oikeioi tou theou; cives sanctorum, et domestici Dei*).

When, in the spirit of the Enlightenment thinkers from whom we are drawing inspiration, Kant was formulating the law of cosmopolitanism, he does not restrict it 'to the conditions of universal hospitality' only. He places on it two limits which doubtless situate a place of reflection and perhaps of transformation or of progress. What are these two limits?

Kant seems at first to extend the cosmopolitan law to encompass universal hospitality *without limit*. Such is the condition of perpetual peace between all men. He expressly determines it as a *natural law* (droit). Being of natural or original derivation, this law would be, therefore, both imprescriptible and inalienable. In the case of natural law, one can recognise within it features of a secularised theological heritage. All human creatures, all finite beings endowed with reason, have received, in equal proportion, 'common possession of the surface of the earth'. No one can in principle, therefore, legitimately appropriate for himself the aforementioned surface (as such, as a *surface-area*) and withhold access to another man. If Kant takes great care to specify that this good or common place covers 'the surface of the earth', it is doubtless so as not to exclude any point of the world or of a spherical and finite globe (globalisation), from which an infinite dispersion remains impossible; but it is above all to expel from it what *is erected, constructed, or what sets itself up above* the soil: habitat, culture, institution, State, etc. All this, even the soil upon which it lies, is no longer soil pure and simple, and, even if founded on the earth, must not be unconditionally accessible to all comers. Thanks to this strictly delimited condition (which is nothing other than the institution of limit as a border, nation, State, public or political space), Kant can deduce two consequences and inscribe two other paradigms upon which it would be in our interest to reflect tomorrow.

1 First of all he excluded hospitality as a *right of residence* (*Gastrecht*); he limits it to the *right of visitation* (*Besuchsrecht*). The right of residence must be made the object of a particular treaty between states. Kant defines thus the conditions that we would have to interpret carefully in order to know how we should proceed:

> We are speaking here, as in the previous articles, not of philanthropy, but of right; and in this sphere hospitality signifies the claim of a stranger entering foreign territory to be treated by its owner without hostility. The latter may send him away again, if this can be done without causing his death; but, so long as he conducts himself peaceably, he must not be treated as an enemy. It is not a right to be treated as a guest to which the stranger can lay claim – a special friendly compact on his behalf would be required to make him for a given time an actual inmate – but he has a right of visitation. This right to present themselves to society belongs to all mankind in virtue of our common right of possession on the surface of the earth on which, as it is a globe, we cannot

be infinitely scattered, and must in the end reconcile ourselves to existence side by side: at the same time, originally no one individual had more right than another to live in any one particular spot.[8]

It is this limitation on the right of residence, as that which is to be made dependent on treaties between states, that perhaps, amongst other things, is what remains for us debatable.

2 By the same token, in defining hospitality in all its rigour as a law (which counts in this respect as progress), Kant assigns to it conditions which make it dependent on state sovereignty, especially when it is a question of the *right of residence*. Hospitality signifies here the *public nature (publicité)* of public space, as is always the case for the juridical in the Kantian sense; hospitality, whether public or private, is dependent on and controlled by the law and the state police. This is of great consequence, particularly for the 'violations of hospitality' about which we have spoken considerably, but just as much for the sovereignty of cities on which we have been reflecting, whose concept is at least as problematic today as in the time of Kant.

All these questions remain obscure and difficult and we must neither conceal them from ourselves nor, for a moment, imagine ourselves to have mastered them. It is a question of knowing how to transform and improve the law, and of knowing if this improvement is possible within an historical space which takes place *between* the Law of an unconditional hospitality, offered *a priori* to every other, to all newcomers, *whoever they may be*, and *the* conditional laws of a right to hospitality, without which *The* unconditional Law of hospitality would be in danger of remaining a pious and irresponsible desire, without form and without potency, and of even being perverted at any moment.

Experience and experimentation thus. Our experience of cities of refuge then will not only be that which cannot wait, but something which calls for an urgent response, a just response, more just in any case than the existing law. An immediate response to crime, to violence, and to persecution. I also imagine the experience of cities of refuge as giving rise to a place (*lieu*) for reflection — for reflection on the questions of asylum and hospitality — and for a new order of law and a democracy to come to be put to the test (*expérimentation*). Being on the threshold of these cities, of these new cities that would be something other than 'new cities', a certain idea of cosmopolitanism, *an other*, has not yet arrived, *perhaps*.

    — If it has (*indeed*) arrived . . .

  — . . . then, one has perhaps not yet recognised it.

NOTES

1 I would like to acknowledge the assistance of Mark Raftery-Skehan with this translation.

2 Hannah Arendt, *The Origins of Totalitarianism* (London: George Allen and Unwin Ltd, 1967), pp. 267–302.

3 Ibid., p. 285. J.D.'s italics.

4 See *Le Monde*, 27 February 1996. See also Luc Legoux, *La Crise d'asile politique en France* (Centre français sur la population et le développement (CEPED)).

5 Ibid., p. xvi.

6 Ibid., p. xviii.

7 Numbers XXXV. 9–32. Cf. I Chronicles 6. 42, 52, where the expression 'Cities of refuge' reappears, and also Joshua 20. 1–9: 'if they admit him

into the city, they will grant him a place where he may live as one of themselves', *Revised English Bible with Apocrypha* (Oxford and Cambridge, 1989), p. 199.

8 In Immanuel Kant, *Perpetual Peace: A Philosophical Essay*, trans. M. Campbell Smith (New York & London, Garland Publishing, Inc., 1972), pp. 137–138.

Part Two
On Forgiveness

Forgiveness

In principle, there is no limit to forgiveness, no *measure*,
no moderation, no 'to what point?'. Provided, of course,
that we agree on some 'proper' meaning of this word.
Now, what do we call 'forgiveness'? What calls for 'forgiveness'? Who calls for, who calls upon forgiveness? It is as
difficult to *measure* an act of forgiveness as it is to take measure
of such questions, for several reasons which I shall quickly
explain.

In the first place, because it is the equivocal which is maintained, especially in today's political debates which reactivate
and displace this notion, the equivocal is maintained
throughout the world. Forgiveness is often confounded,
sometimes in a calculated fashion, with related themes:
excuse, regret, amnesty, prescription, etc.; so many significa-
tions of which certain come under law, a penal law from
which forgiveness must in principle remain heterogeneous
and irreducible.

As enigmatic as the concept of forgiveness remains, it
is the case that the scene, the figure, the language which

'On Forgiveness', © 2001 Studies in Practical Philosophy, translated by
Michael Hughes

27 **On** Cosmopolitanism and Forgiveness

one tries to adapt to it belong to a religious heritage (let's call it Abrahamic, in order to bring together Judaism, the Christianities, and the Islams). This tradition – complex and differentiated, even conflictual – is at once singular and on the way to universalisation through that which a certain theatre of forgiveness puts in place or brings to light.

From this – and this is one of the guiding threads of my seminar on forgiveness (and perjury) – the very dimension of forgiveness tends to efface itself in the course of this globalisation, and with it all measure, any conceptual limit. In all the scenes of repentance, confession, forgiveness, or apology which have multiplied on the geopolitical scene since the last war, and in an accelerated fashion in the past few years, one sees not only individuals, but also entire communities, professional corporations, the representatives of ecclesiastical hierarchies, sovereigns, and heads of state ask for 'forgiveness'. They do this in an Abrahamic language which is not (in the case of Japan or Korea, for example) that of the dominant religion of their society, but which has already become the universal idiom of law, of politics, of the economy, or of diplomacy: at the same time the agent and symptom of this internationalisation. The proliferation of scenes of repentance, or of asking 'forgiveness', signifies, no doubt, a *universal urgency* of memory: it is *necessary* to turn toward the past; and it is *necessary* to take this act of memory, of self-accusation, of 'repentance', of appearance [*comparution*][1] at the same time beyond the juridical instance, or that of the Nation-State. We ask ourselves, then, what happens on this scale. The ways are numerous. One among them consistently leads back to a series of extraordinary events, those which before and during the Second World War made possible, in any case 'authorised', with the Nuremberg Tribunal, the international institution of a juridical concept such as the 'crime against humanity'. There was a 'performative' event of a scope still difficult to interpret.

Even if words like 'crime against humanity' now circulate in everyday language. That event itself was *produced* and author-ised by an international community on a date and according to a figure determined by its history. This overlaps but is not confounded with the history of a reaffirmation of human rights, or a new Declaration of Human Rights. This sort of transformation structured the theatrical space in which the grand forgiveness, the grand scene of repentance which we are concerned with, is played, sincerely or not. Often it has, in its very theatricality, the traits of a grand convulsion – dare we say a frenetic compulsion? No. It also responds, fortunately, to a 'good' movement. However, the simulacra, the automatic ritual, hypocrisy, calculation, or mimicry are often a part, and invite parasites to this ceremony of culpability. Here is a humanity shaken by a movement which would like itself to be unanimous; here is a human race which would claim to accuse itself all at once, publicly and spectacularly, of all the crimes committed in effect by itself against itself, 'against humanity'. For if we were to begin to accuse ourselves, in asking forgiveness, of all the crimes of the past against humanity, there would no longer be an innocent person on earth – and therefore no one in the position to judge or arbitrate. We are all heir, at least, to persons or events marked, in an essential, interior, ineffaceable fashion, by crimes against humanity. Sometimes these events, these massive, organised, cruel murders, which may have been revolutions, great canonic and 'legitimate' Revolutions, were the very ones which permitted the emergence of concepts like those of human rights, or the crime against humanity.

Whether we see here an immense progress, an historic transformation, or a concept still obscure in its limits, fragile in its foundations (or one and the other at the same time – I would lean that way, for my part), this fact cannot be denied: the concept of the 'crime against humanity' remains on the horizon of the entire geopolitics of forgiveness. It furnishes it with its discourse and legitimation. Take the striking example of the Truth and Reconciliation Committee in South Africa. It remains unique despite some analogies, only analogies, some South American precedents, notably in Chile. Well, what gave it its ultimate justification, the declared legitimacy of this commission, is the definition, by the international community in its UN representation, of Apartheid as a 'crime against humanity'.

This convulsion of which I spoke would today take the form of a conversion, of a conversion in fact and tendentially universal: on the way to globalisation. For if, as I believe, the concept of a crime against humanity is the main charge of this self-accusation, of this repenting and this asking forgiveness; if, on the other hand, only a sacredness of the human can, in the last resort, justify this concept (nothing is worse, in this logic, than a crime against the humanity of man and against human rights); if this sacredness finds its meaning in the Abrahamic memory of the religions of the Book, and in a Jewish but above all Christian interpretation of the 'neighbour' or the 'fellow man'; if, from this, the crime against humanity is a crime against what is most sacred in the living, and thus already against the divine in man, in God-made-man or man-made-God-by-God (the death of man and the death of God would here betray the same crime), then the 'globalisation' of forgiveness resembles an immense scene of confession in progress, thus a virtually Christian convulsion-conversion-confession, a process of Christianisation which has no more need for the Christian church.

If, as I was just suggesting, such a language combines and accumulates powerful traditions within it ('Abrahamic' culture and that of a philosophical humanism, and more precisely a cosmopolitanism born from a graft of stoicism with Pauline Christianity), why does it today impose itself on cultures which do not have European or 'biblical' origins? I am thinking of those scenes where a Japanese Prime Minister 'asked forgiveness' of the Koreans and the Chinese for past violence. He presented certain 'heartfelt apologies'[2] in his own name, [at first sight] without implicating the Emperor at the head of state, but a Prime Minister always implicates more than a private person. Recently, there have been real negotiations, this time official and serious, between the Japanese and the South Korean governments on this subject. There will be reparations and a political reorientation. These negotiations, as is almost always the case, aimed at producing a reconciliation (national or international) favourable to a normalisation. The language of forgiveness, at the service of determined finalities, was anything but pure and disinterested. As always in the field of politics.

I shall risk this proposition: each time forgiveness is at the service of a finality, be it noble and spiritual (atonement or redemption, reconciliation, salvation), each time that it aims to re-establish a normality (social, national, political, psychological) by a work of mourning, by some therapy or ecology of memory, then the 'forgiveness' is not pure – nor is its concept. Forgiveness is not, it should not be, normal, normative, normalising. It should remain exceptional and extraordinary, in the face of the impossible: as if it interrupted the ordinary course of historical temporality.

It would be necessary to interrogate from this point of view what is called globalisation, and which I elsewhere[3] call *globalatinisation* – to take into account the effect of Roman Christianity which today overdetermines all language of law, of politics, and even the interpretation of what is called the 'return of the religious'. No alleged disenchantment, no secularisation comes to interrupt it. On the contrary.

II

In order to approach now the very concept of forgiveness, logic and common sense agree for once with the paradox: it is necessary, it seems to me, to begin from the fact that, yes, there is the unforgivable. Is this not, in truth, the only thing to forgive? The only thing that *calls* for forgiveness? If one is only prepared to forgive what appears forgivable, what the church calls 'venial sin', then the very idea of forgiveness would disappear. If there is something to forgive, it would be what in religious language is called mortal sin, the worst, the unforgivable crime or harm. From which comes the aporia, which can be described in its dry and implacable formality, without mercy: forgiveness forgives only the unforgivable. One cannot, or should not, forgive; there is only forgiveness, if there is any, where there is the unforgivable. That is to say that forgiveness must announce itself as impossibility itself. It can only be possible in doing the impossible. For, in this century, monstrous crimes ('unforgivable' then) have not only been committed – which is perhaps itself not so new – but have become visible, known, recounted, named, archived by a 'universal conscience' better informed than ever; because these crimes, at once cruel and massive, seem to escape, or because one has sought to make them escape, in their very excess, from the measure of any human justice, then well, the call to forgiveness finds itself (by the unforgivable itself!) reactivated, remotivated, accelerated.

When the law of 1964 was passed, which determined in France the imprescriptibility of crimes against humanity, a debate was opened. I note in passing that the juridical concept of the *imprescriptible* is in no way equivalent to the non-juridical concept of the unforgivable. One can maintain the imprescriptibility of a crime, give no limit to the duration of an indictment or a possible pursual before the law, while still forgiving the guilty. Inversely, one can acquit or suspend judgement and nevertheless refuse to forgive. It remains that the singularity of the concept of imprescriptibility (by opposition to 'prescription', which has equivalents in other Western systems of law, American law, for example) stems perhaps from what it also introduces, like forgiveness or the unforgivable, a sort of eternity or transcendence, the apocalyptic horizon of a final judgement: in the law beyond the law, in history beyond history. This is a capital and difficult point.

In a polemical text justly entitled 'L'Imprescriptible',

Jankélévitch declares that there would be no question of forgiving crimes against humanity, against the humanity of man: not against 'enemies' (political, religious, ideological), but against that which makes of man a man – that is to say, against the power of forgiveness itself. In an analogous fashion, Hegel, the great thinker of 'forgiveness' and 'reconciliation', said that all is forgivable except the crime against spirit, that is, against the reconciling power of forgiveness. Concerning, of course, the Shoah, Jankélévitch stresses above all another argument, in his eyes decisive: it is even less a question of forgiving in this case, since the criminals did not ask forgiveness. They did not recognise their fault, and manifested no repentance. At least that is, a little quickly perhaps, what Jankélévitch maintains.

However, I would be tempted to contest this conditional logic of the exchange, this presupposition, so widespread, according to which forgiveness can only be considered on the condition that it be asked, in the course of a scene of repentance attesting at once to the consciousness of the fault, the transformation of the guilty, and the at least implicit obligation to do everything to avoid the return of evil. There is here an economic transaction which, at the same time, confirms and contradicts the Abrahamic tradition of which we are speaking. It is important to analyse at its base the tension at the heart of the heritage between, on the one side, the idea which is also a demand for the unconditional, gracious, infinite, aneconomic forgiveness granted to the guilty as guilty, without counterpart, even to those who do not repent or ask forgiveness, and on the other side, as a great number of texts testify through many semantic refinements and difficulties, a conditional forgiveness proportionate to the recognition of the fault, to repentance, to the transformation of the sinner who then explicitly asks forgiveness. And who from that point is no longer guilty through and through, but already another, and better than the guilty one. To this extent, and on this condition, it is no longer the *guilty as such* who is forgiven. One of the questions indissociable from this, and which interests me no less, concerns the essence of the heritage. What does it mean to inherit when the heritage includes an injunction at once double and contradictory? An injunction which it is necessary to reorient, actively and performatively to interpret, but interpreted in obscurity, as if we would have then to reinvent the memory, without pre-established norm or criteria?

Despite my sympathetic admiration for Jankélévitch, and even if I understand what inspires this anger of the just, I have difficulty following it. For example, when he multiplies the imprecations against the good conscience of 'the German', or when he rages against the economic miracle of the Mark and the prosperous obscenity of good conscience, but above all when he justifies the refusal to forgive by the fact, but above all the allegation, of non-repentance. He says, in sum, 'If they had begun in repentance, by asking forgiveness, then we could have conceived granting it to them, but that was not the case.' I have all the more problem following here since in what he himself calls a 'book of philosophy', *Le Pardon*, published earlier, Jankélévitch had been more receptive to the idea of an absolute forgiveness. He claimed at that time a Jewish, and above all Christian, inspiration. He even spoke of an imperative of love and a 'hyperbolic ethics': an ethics, therefore, that carries itself beyond laws, norms, or any obligation. Ethics beyond ethics, there perhaps is the undiscoverable place of forgiveness. Nevertheless, at that moment, and the contradiction thus remains, Jankélévitch did not go so far as to admit an unconditional forgiveness, one which would be granted even to one who did not ask for it.

The core of the argument in 'L'Imprescriptible' and in the section entitled 'To Forgive?' is that the singularity of the Shoah attains the dimension of the *inexpiable*. However, for the inexpiable there is no possible forgiveness according to Jankélévitch, not any forgiveness that would have a meaning [*sens*], that would make sense [*sens*]. For the common or dominant axiom of the tradition, finally, and to my eyes the most problematic, is that *forgiveness must have a meaning*. And this meaning must determine itself on the ground of salvation, of reconciliation, redemption, atonement, I would say even sacrifice. For Jankélévitch, as soon as one can no longer punish the criminal with a 'punishment proportionate to his crime' and 'the punishment becomes almost indifferent' it is a matter of the 'inexpiable' – he says, also, the 'irreparable' (a word that Chirac used in his famous declaration on the crime against the Jews under Vichy: 'France that day performed the irreparable'). From the inexpiable or the irreparable, Jankélévitch concludes the unforgivable. And one does not forgive, according to him, the unforgivable. This connection does not seem to me to follow. For the reason I gave (what would be a forgiveness that forgave only the forgivable?) and because this logic continues to imply that forgiveness remains the correlate to a judgement and the counterpart to a *possible* punishment, to a possible expiation, to the 'expiable'.

Jankélévitch seems to take two things as given (as does Arendt, for example, in *The Human Condition*):

1 Forgiveness must rest on a *human possibility* – I insist on these two words, and above all on the anthropological feature which decides everything (because it will always be about, at the end of it, knowing if forgiveness is a *possibility* or not, or even a faculty, thus a sovereign 'I can', and a human power or not);

2 This human possibility is the correlate to the possibility of punishment – not to avenge oneself, which is something different, to which forgiveness is even more foreign, but to punish according to the law. 'Punishment', says Arendt, 'has something in common with forgiveness, as it tends to put a limit on something that without intervention could continue indefinitely. It is thus very significant; it is a structural element of the domain of *human* [my italics] affairs, that people would be incapable of forgiving what they cannot punish, and that they would be incapable of punishing what reveals itself as unforgivable.'

In 'L'Imprescriptible', therefore, and not in *Le Pardon*, Jankélévitch places himself in that exchange, in that symmetry between punishing and forgiving: forgiveness will no longer have meaning where the crime has become, like the Shoah, 'inexpiable', 'irreparable', out of proportion to all human measure. 'Forgiveness died in the death camps', he says. Yes. Unless it only becomes possible from the moment that it appears impossible. Its history would begin, on the contrary, with the unforgivable.

It is not in the name of an ethical or spiritual purism that I insist on this contradiction at the heart of the heritage, and on the necessity of maintaining the reference to an aneconomical and unconditional forgiveness: beyond the exchange and even the horizon of a redemption or a reconciliation. If I say, 'I forgive you on the condition that, asking forgiveness, you would thus have changed and would no longer be the same', do I forgive? What do I forgive? And whom? What and whom? Something or someone? This is the first syntactic ambiguity which will, be it said, occupy us for a long time. Between the question 'whom?' and the question 'what?'. Does one forgive *something*, a crime, a fault, a wrong, that is to say, an act or a moment which does not exhaust the person incriminated, and at the limit does not become confused with the guilty, who thus remains irreducible to it? Or rather, does one forgive *someone*, absolutely, no longer marking the limit between the injury, the moment of the fault, and on the other side the person taken as responsible or culpable? And in the latter case (the question *'whom?'*) does one ask forgiveness of the victim, or some absolute witness, of God, of such a God, for example, who prescribed forgiving the other (person) in order to merit being forgiven in turn? (The church of France asked forgiveness of God; it did not repent directly or only before people, or before the victims, for example the Jewish community whom they took only as a witness, but publicly it is true, of the forgiveness asked in truth of God, etc.) I must leave these immense questions open.

III

Imagine, then, that I forgive on the condition that the guilty one repents, mends his ways, asks forgiveness, and thus would be changed by a new obligation, and that from then on he would no longer be exactly the same as the one who was found to be culpable. In this case, can one still speak of forgiveness? This would be too simple on both sides: one forgives someone other than the guilty one. In order for there to be forgiveness, must one not on the contrary forgive both the fault and the guilty *as such*, where the one and the other remain as irreversible as the evil, as evil itself, and being capable of repeating itself, unforgivably, without transformation, without amelioration, without repentance or promise? Must one not maintain that an act of forgiveness worthy of its name, if there ever is such a thing, must forgive the unforgivable, and without condition? And that such unconditionality is also inscribed, like its contrary, namely the condition of repentance, in 'our' heritage? Even if this radical purity can seem excessive, hyperbolic, mad? Because if I say, as I think, that forgiveness is mad, and that it must remain a madness of the impossible, this is certainly not to exclude or disqualify it. It is even, perhaps, the only thing that arrives, that surprises, like a revolution, the ordinary course of history, politics, and law. Because that means that it remains heterogeneous to the order of politics or of the juridical as they are ordinarily understood.

One could never, in the ordinary sense of the words, found a politics or law on forgiveness. In all the geopolitical scenes we have been talking about, the word most often abused is 'forgive'. Because it always has to do with negotiations more or less acknowledged, with calculated transactions, with conditions and, as Kant would say, with hypothetical imperatives. These transactions can certainly appear honourable; for example, in the name of 'national reconciliation', the expression to which de Gaulle, Pompidou, and Mitterand, all three, returned at the moment when they believed it necessary to take responsibility in order to efface the debts and crimes of the past, under the Occupation or during the Algerian war. In France, the highest political officials have regularly used the same language: it is necessary to proceed to reconciliation by amnesty, and thus to reconstitute the national unity.

This is a *leitmotiv* of all the French heads of state and Prime Ministers since the Second World War, *without exception*. This was literally the language of those who, after the first moment of purging, decided on the great amnesty of 1951 for the crimes committed under the Occupation. One night I heard (I am citing from memory) Mr Cavaillet say that he had, as a member of parliament, voted for the law of amnesty of 1951 because it was necessary, he said, 'to know how to forget'; above all at that moment, Cavaillet insisted strenuously, that the communist danger was felt to be the most urgent. It was necessary to bring back into the national community all the anti-communists who, collaborators a few years before, risked finding themselves excluded by a law too severe and by a purge not forgetful enough. To repair the national unity meant to re-arm with all available forces in a combat which would continue, this time in a time of peace, or of a war called cold. There is always a strategical or political calculation in the generous gesture of one who offers reconciliation or amnesty, and it is necessary always to integrate this calculation in our analyses. '*National reconciliation*': this was, as I said, the explicit language of de Gaulle when he returned for the first time to Vichy and delivered there a famous discourse on the unity and unicity of France; this was literally the discourse of Pompidou, who also spoke, in a famous press conference, of 'national reconciliation' and of division overcome, when he pardoned Touvier; this was again the language of Mitterand when he maintained, on several occasions, that he was the guarantor of national unity, and very precisely when he refused to declare the culpability of France under Vichy (which he qualified, as you know, as an illegitimate or non-representational power, appropriated by a minority of extremists, although we know the situation to be more complicated, and not only from the formal and legal point of view, but let us leave this). Inversely, when the body of the nation can, without risk, support a minor division, or even finds its unity reinforced by trials, by opening the archives, by the lifting of repression, then, well, other calculations dictate accession to what is called the 'duty of memory' in a more rigorous and public fashion.

It is always the same concern: to see to it that the nation survives its discords, that the traumatisms give way to the work of mourning, and that the Nation-State not be overcome by paralysis. But even where it could be justified, this 'ecological' imperative of social and political health has nothing to do with 'forgiveness', which when spoken of in these terms is taken far too lightly. Forgiveness does not, it should never amount to a therapy of reconciliation. Let us return to the remarkable example of South Africa. Still in prison, Mandela believed that he himself had to assume the decision to negotiate the principle of a procedure of amnesty. First of all, in order to permit the return of the ANC exiles. And in view of a national reconciliation without which the country would have been mired in fire and blood by vengeance. But no more than acquittal, the withdrawal of a case [non-lieu], or even 'grace' (a juridico-political exception we shall speak of again), does amnesty signify 'forgiveness'. However, when Desmond Tutu was named president of the Truth and Reconciliation Commission, he christianised the language of an institution uniquely destined to treat 'politically' motivated crimes (an enormous problem which I will not treat here, just as I will not analyse the complex structure of the aforementioned commission in its comparisons with other juridical instances and penal procedures which are to follow their course). With as much good will as confusion, it seems to me, Tutu, an Anglican archbishop, introduced the vocabulary of repentance and forgiveness. He was reproached for this, among other things, by a non-Christian segment of the black community. Without speaking of the formidable stakes of translation, which I can only evoke here but which, as with the recourse to language itself, concerns the second aspect of your question: is the scene of forgiveness a personal face-to-face, or does it call for some institutional mediation? (And language, the words themselves, are here a first mediating institution.)

In principle, therefore, always in order to follow a vein of the Abrahamic tradition, forgiveness must engage two singularities: the guilty (the 'perpetrator'[4] as they say in South Africa) and the victim. As soon as a third party intervenes, one can again speak of amnesty, reconciliation, reparation, etc., but certainly not of pure forgiveness in the strict sense. The statute of the Truth and Reconciliation Commission is very ambiguous on this subject, as with Tutu's discourse, which oscillates between a non-penal and non-reparative logic of 'forgiveness' (he calls it 'restorative') and a judicial logic of amnesty. We would have to analyse closely the equivocal instability of all of these self-interpretations. Favouring a confusion between the order of forgiveness and the order of justice, but also certainly in abusing their heterogeneity, as well as the fact that the time of forgiveness escapes the judicial process, it is moreover always possible to mimic the scene of 'immediate' and quasi-automatic forgiveness in order to escape justice. The possibility of this calculation always remains open, and one could give many examples of it. And counter examples. Tutu recounts that one day a black woman comes to testify before the Commission. Her husband had been assassinated by torturers who were police officers. She speaks in her language, one of eleven languages officially recognised by the Constitution. Tutu interprets and translates, in his Christian idiom (Anglo-Anglican), something like this: 'A commission or a government cannot forgive. Only I, eventually, could do it. (And I am not ready to forgive.)'[5]

These are very difficult words to hear. This woman victim, this wife of the victim [*Cette femme victime, cette femme de victime*][6] surely wanted to recall that the anonymous body of the State or of a public institution cannot forgive. It has neither the right nor the power to do so; and besides, that would have no meaning. The representative of the State can judge, but forgiveness has precisely nothing to do with judgement. Or even with the public or political sphere. Even if it were 'just', forgiveness would be just of a justice which had nothing to do with judicial justice, with law. There are the courts of justice for that, and these courts never forgive in the strict sense of the word. This woman, perhaps, wanted to suggest something else again: if anyone has the right to forgive, it is only the victim, and not a tertiary institution. For, in addition, even if this spouse is also a victim, well, the absolute victim, if one can say that, remains her dead husband. Only the dead man could legitimately consider forgiveness. The survivor is not ready to substitute herself, abusively, for the dead. The immense and painful experience of the survivor: who would have the right to forgive in the name of the disappeared victims? They are always absent, in a certain way. The *disappeared*, in essence, are themselves never absolutely present, at the moment when forgiveness is asked for, the same as they were at the moment of the crime, and they are sometimes absent in body, often dead.

I will return for a moment to the equivocation of the tradition. Sometimes, forgiveness (given by God, or inspired by divine prescription) must be a gracious gift, without exchange and without condition; sometimes it requires, as its minimal condition, the repentance and transformation of the sinner. What consequence results from this tension? At least this, which does not simplify things: if our idea of forgiveness falls into ruin as soon as it is deprived of its pole of absolute reference, namely its unconditional purity, it remains nonetheless inseparable from what is heterogenous to it, namely the order of conditions, repentance, transformation, as many things as allow it to inscribe itself in history, law, politics, existence itself. These two poles, *the unconditional and the conditional*, are absolutely heterogeneous, and must remain irreducible to one another. They are nonetheless indissociable: if one wants, and it is necessary, forgiveness to become effective, concrete, historic; if one wants it to *arrive*, to happen by changing things, it is necessary that this purity engage itself in a series of conditions of all kinds (psycho-sociological, political, etc.). It is between these two poles, *irreconcilable but indissociable*, that decisions and responsibilities are to be taken. Yet despite all the confusions which reduce forgiveness to amnesty or to amnesia, to acquittal or prescription, to the work of mourning or some political therapy of reconciliation, in short to some historical ecology, it must never be forgotten, nevertheless, that all of that refers to a certain idea of pure and unconditional forgiveness, without which this discourse would not have the least meaning. What complicates the question of 'meaning' is again what I suggested a moment ago: pure and unconditional forgiveness, in order to have its own meaning, must have no 'meaning', no finality, even no intelligibility. It is a madness of the impossible. It would be necessary to follow, without letting up, the consequence of this paradox, or this aporia.

What is called the *right of grace* gives an example of this, at once an example among others and the exemplary model. For, if it is true that forgiveness would have to remain heterogeneous to the juridico-political, judicial, or penal order; if it is true that it should, each time, in each occurrence, remain an absolute exception, then there is an exception of some sort to that law of exception; and in the West it is precisely this theological tradition which accords to the sovereign an exorbitant right. For the right of grace is, as its name suggests, of the order of law, but a law which inscribes in the laws a power above the laws.[7] The absolute monarch can, by divine right, pardon a criminal; that is to say, exercise in the name of the State a forgiveness that transcends and neutralises the law. Right [droit] beyond the law [droit]. As with the very idea of the sovereign, this right of grace has been reappropriated into the republican heritage. In modern States of the democratic sort, such as France, one would say that it has been secularised (if this word has a meaning other than in the religious tradition that it maintains in claiming to escape it). In others, such as the United States, the secularisation is not even a simulacrum, since the President and governors, who have the right of grace (pardon, clemency[8]), first take an oath on the Bible, use religious language in official discourse, and invoke the name or benediction of God each time they address the nation. What counts in this absolute exception of the right of grace is that the exception from the law, the exception to the law, is situated at the summit or at the foundation of the juridico-political. In the body of the sovereign, it incarnates what founds or supports or establishes, at the top, with the unity of the nation, the guarantee of the constitution, the conditions and exercise of the law. As is always the case, the transcendental principle of a system doesn't belong to the system. It is as foreign to it as an exception.

Without contesting the principle of this right of grace, the most 'elevated' there is, the most noble but also the most 'slippery' and the most equivocal, the most dangerous and the most arbitrary, Kant recalls the strict limitation which would be necessary to impose upon it so that it would not give way to the worst injustices: that the sovereign could pardon only where the crime concerns himself (and thus concerns, in his body, the very guarantee of the law, of the rule of law [Etat de droit] and of the State). As in the Hegelian logic we spoke of above, nothing is impardonable but the crime against that which gives the power to forgive, the crime against forgiveness, in sum – the spirit according to Hegel, and what he calls 'the Spirit of Christianity' – but it is precisely this unforgivable, and this unforgivable alone which the sovereign would still have the right to forgive, and only when the 'body of the king' in his sovereign function is threatened through the other 'body of the king' which is here the 'same', the singular and empirical body of flesh. Outside this absolute exception, in all other cases, wherever the harms concern the subjects themselves, which is to say almost always, the right of grace could not be exercised without injustice. In fact, one knows that it is always exercised in a conditional manner, in the function of an interpretation or a calculation on the part of the sovereign regarding what joins a particular interest (his own, those of his family, or those of a fraction of society) and the interest of the State. A recent example of this was given by Clinton – who has never been inclined to pardon anyone and who is a rather offensive partisan of the death penalty. However, using his 'right to pardon' he recently pardoned the Puerto Ricans imprisoned for a long time for terrorism. Well, the Republicans did not fail to contest this absolute privilege of the executive in accusing the President of wanting to help Hillary Clinton in her upcoming electoral campaign in New York, where Puerto Ricans are, as you know, numerous.

IV

In the case at once exceptional and exemplary of the right of grace, where what exceeds the juridico-political inscribes itself in the constitutional law in order to found itself; well, *there is and there is not* this personal head-to-head or face-to-face, which one could think is required by the very essence of forgiveness. Even there, where it should engage only absolute singularities, it cannot *manifest* itself in some fashion without calling on a third, the institution, sociality, the transgenerational heritage, on the survivor in general; and first on that universalising instance which is language. Can there be, in one way or another, a scene of forgiveness without a shared language? This sharing is not only that of a national language or an idiom, but that of an agreement on the meanings of words, their connotations, rhetoric, the aim of a reference, etc. It is here another form of the same aporia: when the victim and the guilty share no language, when nothing common and universal permits them to understand one another, forgiveness seems deprived of meaning; it is certainly a case of the absolutely unforgivable, that impossibility of forgiveness, of which we just said nevertheless that it was, paradoxically, the very element of all possible forgiveness. For forgiveness it is necessary *on the one hand* to understand, on both sides, the nature of the fault, to know who is guilty of what evil toward whom, etc. Already a very improbable thing. Because you imagine a 'logic of the unconscious' would come to disturb this 'knowledge', and all the schemas for which it nevertheless holds a 'truth'. And you imagine also what would happen when the same perturbation made everything tremble, when it came to affect the 'work of mourning', the therapy of which we spoke, and law and politics. For, if a pure forgiveness cannot, if it *must* not *present itself* as such, and thus exhibit itself in consciousness without at the same time denying itself, betraying or reaffirming a sovereignty, then how to know what is an act of forgiveness, if it never takes place, and who forgives whom, or what from whom? For, *on the other hand*, if it is necessary, as we just said, that the two sides must agree on the nature of the fault, must know consciously who is guilty of which evil toward whom, etc., and if the thing remains very improbable, the contrary is also true. At the same time, it is necessary in effect that alterity, non-identification, even incomprehension, remain irreducible. Forgiveness is thus mad. It must plunge, but lucidly, into the night of the unintelligible. Call this the unconscious or the non-conscious if you want. As soon as the victim 'understands' the criminal, as soon as she exchanges, speaks, agrees with him, the scene of reconciliation has commenced, and with it this ordinary forgiveness which is anything but forgiveness. Even if I say 'I do not forgive you' to someone who asks my forgiveness, but whom I understand and who understands me, then a process of reconciliation has begun; the third has intervened. Yet, this is the end of pure forgiveness.

There could be, in effect, all sorts of proximity (where the crime is between people who know each other): language, neighbourhood, familiarity, even family, etc. But in order for evil to emerge, 'radical evil' and perhaps worse again, the unforgivable evil, the only one which would make the question of forgiveness emerge, it is necessary that at the most intimate of that intimacy an absolute hatred would come to interrupt the peace. This destructive hostility can only aim at what Levinas calls the 'face' of the Other, the similar other, the closest neighbour, between the Bosnians and Serbs, for example, within the same quarter, the same house, sometimes in the same family. Must forgiveness saturate the abyss? Must it suture the wound in a process of reconciliation? Or rather give place to another peace, without forgetting, without amnesty, fusion, or confusion? Of course, no one would decently dare to object to the imperative of reconciliation. It would be better to put an end to the crimes and discords. Once again, however, I believe it necessary to distinguish between forgiveness and this process of reconciliation, this reconstitution of a health or a 'normality', as necessary and desirable as it would appear through amnesties, the 'work of mourning', etc. A 'finalised' forgiveness is not forgiveness; it is only a political strategy or a psycho-therapeutic economy. In Algeria today, despite the infinite suffering of the victims, and the irreparable harm they suffer for ever, one can certainly think that the survival of the country, the society, the State, is coming about by the process of announced reconciliation. One can, from this point of view, 'understand' that a vote would have approved the politics promised by Bouteflika. However, I believe that the word 'forgiveness' which was pronounced on that occasion was inappropriate, in particular by the Algerian head of state. I find it unjust at once with respect to the victims of atrocious crimes (no head of state has the right to forgive in their place) and with respect to the meaning [sens] of this word, the non-negotiable, aneconomic, apolitical, non-strategic unconditionality that it prescribes. Once again, however, this respect for the word or the concept does not only translate a semantic or philosophical purism. All sorts of unacknowledgeable 'politics', all sorts of strategic ruses can hide themselves abusively behind a 'rhetoric' or a 'comedy' of forgiveness, in order to avoid the step of the law. When politics has to do with analysing, judging, that is, counteracting these abuses practically, conceptual exigence is necessary, even where it takes into account the paradoxes and aporias, by accepting the burden and declaring them. It is, once again, the condition of responsibility.

I remain 'torn' (between a 'hyberbolic' ethical vision of forgiveness, pure forgiveness, and the reality of a society at work in pragmatic processes of reconciliation). But without power, desire, or need to decide. The two poles are irreducible to one another, certainly, but they remain indissociable. In order to inflect politics, or what you just called the 'pragmatic processes', in order to change the law (which, thus, finds itself between the two poles, the 'ideal' and the 'empirical' – and what is more important to me here is, between these two, this universalising mediation, this history of the law, the possibility of this progress of the law), it is necessary to refer to a ' "hyperbolic" ethical vision of forgiveness'. Even if I were not sure of the words 'vision' or 'ethics' in this case, let us say that only this inflexible exigence can orient a history of laws, and evolution of the law. It alone can inspire here, now, in the urgency, without waiting, response and responsibilities.

V

Let us return to the question of *human rights*, of the concept of *crime against humanity*, but also of *sovereignty*. More than ever, these three motifs are connected in the public sphere and in political discourse. Even if a certain notion of sovereignty is often positively associated with the right of the person, with the right to self-determination, with the ideal of emancipation, in truth with the very idea of freedom, with the principle of human rights, it is often in the name of human rights, and to punish or prevent crimes against humanity that we come to limit or at least to imagine limiting the sovereignty of certain Nation-States. But of certain ones among them more than others. Recent examples: the interventions in Kosovo, or East Timor, otherwise different in their nature and aim. (The case of the Gulf War is complicated in a different way: the sovereignty of Iraq is limited today, but after having claimed to defend, against it, the sovereignty of a small State – and in the process several other interests, but let's move on.) Let us always be attentive, as Hannah Arendt recalls so lucidly, that this limitation of sovereignty is only imposed where it is 'possible' (physically, militarily, economically), that is to say always imposed on small, relatively weak States by powerful States. The latter remain jealous of their own sovereignty in limiting those of others. It also weighs in a determinate fashion on the decisions of international institutions. It is there an order and a 'state of fact' which could be either consolidated to the service of the 'strong' or, on the contrary, little by little, dismantled, put in crisis, menaced by concepts (that is to say here by instituted performatives, by events in essence historical and transformable), like those of new 'human rights' or of 'crime against humanity', by conventions on genocide, torture, or terrorism. Between the two hypotheses, all depends on the politics that puts these concepts to work. Despite their ageless roots and foundations, these concepts are entirely young, at least as mechanisms of international law. And when, in 1964 – it was yesterday – France judged it opportune to decide that the crimes against humanity were to remain imprescriptible (a decision which made possible all the trials that you know – yesterday again, the Papon trial), in this it implicitly called on a sort of beyond the law in the law. The imprescriptible, as a juridical notion, is certainly not the unforgivable; we have just seen why. But the imprescriptible, I come back to this, signals toward the transcendent order of the unconditional, of forgiveness and the unforgivable, toward a sort of ahistoricity, even eternity and the Final Judgement, goes beyond history and the finite time of the law: for ever, 'eternally', everywhere and always, a crime against humanity will always be subject to judgment, and it will never be effaced from the judicial archive. It is therefore a certain idea of forgiveness and the unforgivable, of a certain beyond of the law (beyond all historical determination of the law) which inspired the legislators and the members of parliament, those who produce the law, when, for example, they instituted in France the imprescriptibility of crimes against humanity or, in a more general fashion, when they transform international law and install universal courts. This shows well that, despite its theoretical, speculative, purist, abstract appearance, any reflection on an unconditional exigency is engaged in advance, and thoroughly in a concrete history. It can induce processes of transformation – political, juridical, but in truth without limit.

That said, since I am split between these apparently insoluble difficulties, I am tempted by two types of response. On the one hand, there is, there has to be, it must be accepted, the 'insoluble'. In politics and beyond. When the givens of a problem or a task do not appear as infinitely contradictory, placing me before the aporia of a double injunction, then I know in advance what it is necessary to do, I believe the knowledge, this knowledge commands and programmes the action: it is done, there is no more decision or responsibility to take. On the contrary, a certain non-knowledge must leave me disarmed before what I have to do so that I have to do it in order for me to feel freely obligated and bound to respond to it. I must then, and only then, respond to this transaction between two contradictory and equally justified imperatives. Not that it is necessary *not to know*. On the contrary, it is necessary to know the most and the best possible, but between the widest, the most refined, the most necessary knowledge, and the responsible decision, an abyss remains, and must remain. We find here again the distinction between the two orders (indissociable but heterogeneous) which has preoccupied us since the beginning of this interview. *On the other hand*, if 'politics' is what you designate in speaking of 'pragmatic processes of reconciliation', then, taking seriously these political urgencies, I believe also that we are not defined through and through by the political, and above all not by citizenship, by the statutory belonging to a Nation-State. Must we not accept that, in heart or in reason, above all when it is a question of 'forgiveness', something arrives which exceeds all institution, all power, all juridico-political authority? We can imagine that someone, a victim of the worst, himself, a member of his family, in his generation or the preceding, demands that justice be done, that the criminals appear before a court, be judged and condemned by a court – and yet in his heart forgives.

VI

The inverse, of course, is also true. We can imagine, and accept, that someone would never forgive, even after a process of acquittal or amnesty. The secret of this experience remains. It must remain intact, inaccessible to law, to politics, even to morals: absolute. But I would make of this trans-political principle a political principle, a political rule or position taking: it is necessary also in politics to respect the secret, that which exceeds the political or that which is no longer in the juridical domain. This is what I would call the 'democracy to come'. In the radical evil of which we are speaking, and consequently in the enigma of the forgiveness of the unforgivable, there is a sort of 'madness' which the juridico-political cannot approach, much less appropriate. Imagine a victim of terrorism, a person whose children have been deported or had their throats cut, or another whose family was killed in a death oven. Whether she says 'I forgive' or 'I do not forgive', in either case I am not sure of understanding. I am even sure of not understanding, and in any case I have nothing to say. This zone of experience remains inaccessible, and I must respect its secret. What remains to be done, then, publicly, politically, juridically, also remains difficult. Let us take again the example of Algeria. I understand, I share the same desire as those who say: 'We must make peace, it is necessary that the nation survive, that's enough of these monstrous murders, we must do what is necessary for this to stop.' And if, for that, it is necessary to trick, even to the point of lying or confusion (as when Bouteflika said: *'We will free the political prisoners who do not have blood on their hands'*), well, go for that abusive rhetoric, it will not have been the first time in recent history, in less recent and above all the colonial history of this country. I understand, then, this 'logic', but I also understand the opposed logic which refuses at all cost, and on principle, this useful mystification. Well, here is the most difficult moment, the law of the responsible transaction. According to the situations and according to the moments, the responsibilities to be taken are different. It seems to me that what they are now preparing to do in Algeria should not be done in the France of today. The French society of today can permit itself to bring to light, with an inflexible rigour, all the crimes of the past (including those which continue in Algeria, precisely, and the thing is not yet done), it can judge them and not let the memory fade. There are situations where, on the contrary, it is necessary, if not to let the memory fade (that should never be necessary, where possible), but at least to act as if, on the public scene, it was renounced to draw all the consequences from it. One is never sure of making the just choice; one never knows, one will never know with what is called knowledge. The future will give us no more knowledge, because it itself will have been determined by that choice. It is here that responsibilities are to be re-evaluated at each moment, according to concrete situations, that is to say, those that do not wait, those that do not give us time for infinite deliberation. The response cannot be the same in Algeria today, yesterday, or tomorrow, and in the France of 1945, 1968–70, or of the year 2000. It is more than difficult; it is infinitely distressing. It is night. But to recognise these 'contextual' differences is an entirely different thing from an empiricist, relativist, or pragmatist resignation. Precisely because the difficulty emerges in the name of and because of unconditional principles, it is therefore irreducible to these simplicities (empiricist, relativist, or pragmatist). In any case, I would not reduce the terrible question of the word 'forgiveness' to these 'processes' in which it finds itself engaged in advance, as complex and inevitable as they may be.

All Nation-States are born and found themselves in violence. I believe that truth to be irrecusable. Without even exhibiting atrocious spectacles on this subject, it suffices to underline a law of structure: the moment of foundation, the instituting moment, is anterior to the law or legitimacy which it founds. It is thus *outside the law*, and violent by that very fact. But you know that this abstract truth could be illustrated (what a word, here!) by terrifying documents, and from the history of all States, the oldest and the youngest. Before the modern forms of what is called, in the strict sense, 'colonialism', all States (I would dare to say, without playing too much with the word and etymology, all *cultures*) have their origin in an aggression of the *colonial* type. This foundational violence is not only forgotten. The foundation is made *in order to* hide it; by its essence it tends to organise amnesia, sometimes under the celebration and sublimation of the grand beginnings. However, what appears singular and new today is the *project* of making States, or at least of heads of state in title (Pinochet), and even of current heads of state (Milosevic), appear before universal authorities. It has to do only with projects or hypotheses, but this possibility suffices to announce a transformation: it constitutes in itself a major event. The sovereignty of the State, the immunity of a head of state are no longer in principle, in law, untouchable. Of course, numerous equivocations will remain for a long time, before which it is necessary to redouble vigilance. We are far from taking action and putting these projects to work, because international law still depends too much on sovereign and powerful Nation-States. What's more, when one takes action, in the name of universal human rights or against 'crimes against humanity', one often does it in an interested fashion, taking into account complex and sometimes contradictory strategies, at the mercy of States not only jealous of their own sovereignty, but dominant on the international scene, pressed to intervene here rather than there, for example in Kosovo rather than in Chechnya, to limit it to recent examples, etc., and excluding, to be sure, all intervention in their own affairs. This explains, for example, the hostility of China to all interference of this type in Asia, in Timor, for example – this could give rise to ideas concerning Tibet; or again the reticence of the United States, even of France, but also of certain 'Southern' countries before the universal powers (jurisdiction, competence) promised to the International Criminal Court, etc.

VII

One returns regularly to this history of sovereignty. And since we are speaking of forgiveness, what makes the 'I forgive you' sometimes unbearable or odious, even obscene, is the affirmation of sovereignty. It is often addressed from the top down, it confirms its own freedom or assumes for itself the power of forgiving, be it as victim or in the name of the victim. However, it is also necessary to think about an absolute victimisation which deprives the victim of life, or the right to speak, or that freedom, that force and that power which *authorises*, which permits the accession to the position of 'I forgive'. There, the unforgivable would consist of depriving the victim of this right to speech, of speech itself, of the possibility of all manifestation, of all testimony. The victim would then be a victim, in addition, of seeing himself stripped of the minimal, elementary *possibility* of *virtually* considering forgiving the unforgivable. This absolute crime does not only occur in the form of murder.

An immense difficulty, then. Each time forgiveness is effectively exercised, it seems to suppose some sovereign power. That could be the sovereign power of a strong and noble soul, but also a power of State exercising an uncontested legitimacy, the power necessary to organise a trial, an applicable judgement or, eventually, acquittal, amnesty, or forgiveness. If, as Jankélévitch and Arendt claim (I have given my reservations on this subject), one only forgives where one can judge and punish, therefore evaluate, then the putting into place, the institution of an instance of judgement, supposes a power, a force, a sovereignty. You know the 'revisionist' argument: the Nuremberg Tribunal was the invention of the victors; it remained at their disposition to establish the law, judge and condemn, as well as to pronounce innocence, etc.

What I dream of, what I try to think as the 'purity' of a forgiveness worthy of its name, would be a forgiveness without power: *unconditional but without sovereignty*. The most difficult task, at once necessary and apparently impossible, would be to dissociate *unconditionality* and *sovereignty*. Will that be done one day? It is not around the corner, as is said. But since the hypothesis of this unpresentable task announces itself, be it as a dream for thought, this madness is perhaps not so mad . . .

NOTES

1 The French word *comparution* has the sense of an appearance before a judge in a court of law.

2 In English in the original.

3 NDLR. cf. 'Foi et savoir, les deux sources de la "religion" aux limites de la simple raison', in J. Derrida and G. Vattimo, *La Religion*, Le Seuil, 1996.

4 In English in the original.

5 In English in the original.

6 There would be much to say here about sexual differences, having to do with the victims or their testimony. Tutu relates also how certain women forgave in the presence of the executioners. But Antje Krog, in an admirable book, *The Country of My Skull*, describes the situation of militant women who, raped and then accused by the torturers of being not militants but whores, could not testify about this before the commission, or even in their family, without baring themselves, without showing their scars or without exposing themselves one more time, by their very testimony, to another violence. The 'question of forgiveness' cannot even be posed publicly to these women, some of whom now occupy high positions in the State. There exists a 'Gender Commission' on this subject in South Africa.

7 'Car le droit de grâce est bien, comme son nom l'indique, de l'ordre du droit mais d'un droit qui inscrit dans les lois un pouvoir au-dessus des lois.' As is often noted, the word *droit* in French has the meaning of both 'law' and 'right'. Trans.

8 In English in the original.